to J. Laughlin

**Books by Denise Levertov**

*Poetry*

**The Double Image**

**Here and Now**

**Overland to the Islands**

**With Eyes at the Back of Our Heads**

**The Jacob's Ladder**

**O Taste and See**

**The Sorrow Dance**

**Relearning the Alphabet**

**To Stay Alive**

**Footprints**

*Translations*

**Guillevic/ Selected Poems**

Denise
Levertov

# Footprints

A New Directions Book

Library of Congress Catalog Card Number: 72–80972



ACKNOWLEDGMENTS

Some of these poems first appeared in the following publications: *Abraxas, The Amphora, Athanor, Citizen of the Imagination, Damascus Road, Decal Review, Earth's Daughters, Field, Hanging Loose, Lillabulero, Madrona, Manroot, Mill Mountain Review, The North American Review, Poems from Summer Poems, Poetry, Poetry Review, Quetzal, The Record, Red Clay Reader, Rogue River Gorge, The Round Table, The Southern Review, Sumac, Voices from Earth.*

"Living with a Painting" first appeared in *Poetry.*

First published clothbound and as ND Paperbook 344 in 1972
Published simultaneously in Canada by McClelland & Stewart, Ltd.

Manufactured in the United States of America

New Directions Books are published for James Laughlin
by New Directions Publishing Corporation,
333 Sixth Avenue, New York 10014

## Contents

## The Footprints

*Someone crossed this field last night:*
*day reveals*
*a perspective of lavender caves*
*across the snow.        Someone*
*entered the dark woods.*

## Hut

Mud and wattles.        Round almost.
Moss. Threshold: a writing,
small stones inlaid, footworn.
'Enter, who
so desires.'

Floor, beaten earth.        Walls
shadows.        Ashpit at center.
By day, coming in from
molten green, dusk
profound.        By night, through smokehole,
the star.

## A Defeat in the Green Mountains

*(Memory of Summer, 1955)*

On a dull day she goes
to find the river,
accompanied by two
unwilling children, shut in
among thorns, vines, the
long grass

stumbling, complaining, the
blackflies biting them,
but persists, drawn
by river-sound close beyond
the baffling scratchy thicket

and after a half-hour they emerge
upon the water
                    flowing by
both dark and clear.
          A space and
          a movement crossing
          their halted movement.
But the river is deep

the mud her foot stirs up
frightens her; the kids are
scared and angry. No way
to reach the open fields over there.
Back then:
swamp underfoot, through the

perverse thickets, finding
a path finally to the
main road—defeated,
to ponder the narrow
depth of the river,
its absorbed movement past her.

## The Rebuff

Yes, I'm nettled.
I touched a leaf
because I like to touch leaves
(even though this one
as it happens, had nothing
of special grace, no shine)

and though it had no spikes,
or thorns attached to it,
nothing like that
to warn the hand,
here I am tingling, it
hurts. I must look

for the coarse, patient
dockleaves nearby,
faithfully awaiting
nettled hands
to soothe with their juice,
wasted otherwise.

## Living with a Painting

*for Albert Kresch*

It ripens
while I sleep, afternoons, on the old sofa,

the forms ready themselves for dazed, refreshed,
wakening senses to bite on,
'taste with the mind's tongue.'

Yes, that confusion
comes of sleep, and all was ripe
before, and I green.
Yet it's true
'One who makes it, and one who needs it.'

The work ripens
within the temper of living round about it,
that brings as tribute, as rain,
many awakenings

until a once-cold
arbitrary violet reveals itself
as radiance, a defining halo

and discovered
geometries in interplay

show in their harvest-time
vase, lute, beaker.

*1962*

## An Old Friend's Self-Portrait

i

Somber, the mouth pinched and twisted,
eyes half-fierce, half-sad,
the portrait of my old friend stares at me
or at the world; that face
I remember as it laughed
twenty years ago, not untroubled but
more certain, face of an artist who
now with a master's hand paints
the image of his own
in-sight.

ii

Strong, the brow
revealed in volume, the ears
listening,
the eyes
watching time purse the
gentle smiling lips I remember,
this face
writes itself on triple-S board,
signs itself in thick
ridges of paint,
breaks through the mirror.

*1970*

*In love* (unless loved) is not *love.*
You're right: x needs–

with azure sparks down dazedly
drifting through vast night
long after–

                the embrace of y to even
begin to become z.
                To x alone
something else happens. Example:

a woman painter returns,
younger than she should be, from travels
in monotone countries

and on arrival, bandages of fatigue
whipped off her eyes,
                instantly
looks, looks at whose shadow
first falls on her primed (primal) canvas
(all the soul she has left
for the moment)–:

At once the light
(not the gray north of journeys)
colors him! Candle-gold,

yet not still, but shivering,
lit white flesh for her (who preferred brown)
and hair light oak or walnut
was mahogany on the dream-palette.

Setting to work, the painter
paints what she sees: the object
moves, her eyes change focus
faithfully, the nimbus
dances.

All one year she paints:
the works are known later by titles—
'Fiery Clouds,' 'Alembic,' '*Du Bleu Noir,*' 'The Burning-Glass.'
Rectangles, ovals, all the landscapes are portraits,
x kneels at the feet of y, barbaric frankincense
enclouds her. But y, embarrassed,
and finally indifferent, turns
away. Talking (he is a poet)

talking, walking away, entering
a small boat, the middle distance,

sliding downstream away.
She has before her

a long scroll to paint on, but no room
to follow that river.           The light's going.

'*L'homme est un drôle de corps,*
*qui n'a pas son centre de gravité en lui-même,*'
she reads, pages falling from trees
at need around her.           She continues

to paint what she saw:

y is a brushstroke now
in furthest perspective, it hurts

the eyes in dusk to see it, no one,
indeed, will know that speck of fire

but x herself, who has not
(in this example) even begun to become

z, but remains
x, a painter; though not perhaps
unchanged. Older. We'll take

some other symbol to represent
*that* difference—a or o.

*June, 1969*

## Intrusion

After I had cut off my hands
and grown new ones

something my former hands had longed for
came and asked to be rocked.

After my plucked out eyes
had withered, and new ones grown

something my former eyes had wept for
came asking to be pitied.

*August, 1969*

## Overheard over S. E. Asia

'White phosphorus, white phosphorus,
mechanical snow,
where are you falling?'

'I am falling impartially on roads and roofs,
on bamboo thickets, on people.
My name recalls rich seas on rainy nights,
each drop that hits the surface eliciting
luminous response from a million algae.
My name is a whisper of sequins. Ha!
Each of them is a disk of fire,
I am the snow that burns.
                                        I fall
wherever men send me to fall—
but I prefer flesh, so smooth, so dense:
I decorate it in black, and seek
the bone.'

## Scenario

The theater of war. Offstage
a cast of thousands weeping.

Left center, well-lit, a mound
of unburied bodies,

or parts of bodies. Right,
near some dead bamboo that serves as wings,

a whole body, on which
a splash of napalm is working.

Enter the Bride.

She has one breast, one eye,
half of her scalp is bald.

She hobbles towards center front.
Enter the Bridegroom,

a young soldier, thin, but without
visible wounds. He sees her.

Slowly at first, then faster and faster,
he begins to shudder, to shudder,

to ripple with shudders.            Curtain.

## Time to Breathe

*(Adapted from a prose poem*
*by Jean-Pierre Burgart)*

Evenings enduring, blending
one with the next. Ocean calmly
rocking reflected docks and those
indecipherable roads that
inscribe themselves in sky
way above trajectories of the swifts.

That freshness, over
and over: summer
in folds of your dress, mysterious fabric.
And in the disturbing
gentle grace of your neck.
The same summer shadow
looking out of your eyes.

Night seems to stop short
at the horizon. Perhaps it never
will quite arrive. Perhaps,
renewed in the breath of these
first summer days,
we shall leave off dying.

## Hope It's True

Wonder if this very day the Hunza
are leading their charmed lives.
Their limbs anointed with oil of apricot,
are they singing, walking the
high paths? Himalayan
blues you couldn't
cry to, it's
like almond milk, sesame, such goodness,
the blues of joy?

While Nevada whores wake anxious
at airconditioned noon,
figuring a blast some time
may shatter the casinos . . .
While Mississippi babies grunt and die,
tired of hunger
and 'small clashes' rip human guts per
daily usual, closer to Hunza-land than here . . .
While an absurd flag
clatters in dust of lunar winds . . .

is the royal apricot-taster
even now stepping sideways from tree to tree
to check on bitterness?—that no Hunza,
the length of the land, shall eat sorrow?

*July, 1969*

## M.C. 5

*for John Sinclair*

Not to blow the mind but
focus it again, renew its
ferocious innocence, hot-pepper sting of
wonder, impatient love.

Enough energy
to save the world; could be.
'Come Together' winds down,
grimly slow-spiralling,
                                        only to recoil
with a snap! We're off!
Some zephyr rising
from choppy seas
        charges itself, lifts to a steady
        sweep, it picks me up, it
picks us up, lift up your heads
O ye gates.

(World's heart
keeps skipping a beat,
sweat crawls on the moon's white
stony face.
                    Life's
winding down.) Tighten the spring.
Something is breathing deep. Ozone, oxygen.
Even yet. Kick out the jams.

*July 30, 1969*

## Love Poem

*for Mitch*

Swimming through dark, slow,
breaststroke—
                    not to startle
                    walls or chairs and
                    wake you—
I almost sundered the
full to the brim with moonlight
mirror

*September, 1969*

## A Place to Live

Honeydew seeds: on impulse
strewn in a pot of earth. Now,

(the green vines) wandering
down over the pot's edges:

certainly no room here to lay
the egg of a big, pale,
green-fleshed melon.
                              Wondering

where the hell to go.

## The News

East Boston too, like the fields
somewhere, from which the snow's
      melting to show forth black
      earth and timid
      tips of grass, is preparing
for spring. In the windows
of candy stores are displayed
jump-ropes: white cord and glossy
red-and-green handles.

## Obstinate Faith

Branch-lingering oakleaves, dry
brown over gray snowglare,
make of a gust of wind
an instrument, to play
'spring rain.'

## Fragment

Not free to love where their liking chooses,
lacking desire for what love proposes,
they wander indoors and out, calling
'Eros, Eros' to the winged one,
who will not listen, for he will bear no bondage . . .

Gary with deer and bear
in the Sierras, in poems.
Acting his dreams out:
kind man,
practical.
Knows
how to kill and skin deer
and how to eat them
and love their life,
love them to life.
Daily his year-old son
runs out to greet them, they browse
deep in his green,
he knows them.

And another Gary
(McDonald) in
New Britain, dreams me
                        a letter to live from–
that day's bread:
'I am just
thinking, writing, breathing here,
phantom of air . . . the
face of the world is
a million eyes.'
Wakes me to know
'there is a way
to the journey. A love grows into itself.'

And a third
(Aspenberg) planning
a Chronicle of the
End of the World, meanwhile
reads my chart: 'Many
loves at first sight.

Visions are presented.
You must choose
the worthy ones to follow.
Your death
may come in a
public place . . .'

'Horoscopes,' he says, 'would make
perfect poems if I could get into them.
Everything relates to all.'

## Under a Blue Star

*Under a blue star, dragon*          *of skygate . . .*
Such wakenings into twilight, foreboding intermingled
with joy, beyond
hope of knowledge. The days
a web of wires, of energies vibrating
in chords and single
long notes of song; but nights
afloat on dream, dreams
that float silent, or leave word
of blue sky-dragons, to seduce
the day's questions, drown them
in twilight before dawn . . . What gate
opens, dim there in the mind's
field, river-mists of the sky
veiling its guardian?

## Exchange

Sea gulls inland.
Come for a change of diet,
a breath of
earth-air.

I smell the
green, dank, amber, soft
undersides of an old pier in their cries.

## 3 a.m., September 1, 1969

*for Kenneth Rexroth*

Warm wind, the leaves
rustling without dryness,
hills dissolved into silver.

It could be any age,
four hundred years ago or a time
of post-revolutionary peace,
the rivers clean again, birth rate and crops
somehow in balance . . .

In heavy dew
under the moon the blond grasses
lean in swathes on the field slope. Fervently
the crickets practice their religion of ectasy.

## A New Year's Garland for My Students/ MIT: 1969–70

### i Arthur

In winter, intricately wrapped, the buds
of trees and bushes
are firm and small and go unnoticed,
though their complexity is as beautiful
now as eventual
                    silky leaves in spring.

### ii Barry

What task is it
hidden just beyond vision yet,
your frown tries
to touch, as if
there, almost within
reach of
your eyes' blue light, as if
frowning were weight that
would pin phantoms to the
ground of
knowledge–
                What Gorgon is it
that shall be given you
(revealed)
            to strike?

## iii Bill

There is a fence around the garden
but the gate stands open.

And the garden within
is pleasant–
neither drearily formal
nor sad with neglect:

oldfashioned, with shade-trees and places
to take the sun, with paths
planted with fragrant resilient herbs.

But looking
out of the thickest, darkest branches–
back of the stone pool,
behind the arbor–

eyes of some animal:

blue-green gray, are they?
Topaz?
          They question
and propose

no answers yet; disquieting
in the still garden,
and disquieted.

## iv Don

If the body is a house,
the house a temple,

in that temple
is a labyrinth,

in that labyrinth's core
a vast room,

in the room's remote depths
an altar,

upon the altar
a battle raging, raging,

between two angels, one feathered
with spines, with sharp flames,

one luminous, the subtle
angel of understanding,

and from time to time a smile flickers
on the face of the mean angel

and slips, shadowy, over
to the gentle face.

## v **Ernie**

Hey Ernie, here you come suavely
round the corner in your
broken-windowed bus
and brake elegantly and swing
open the door so I can get in and ride on, sitting
on crumpled poems among guitars and
percussion sets.
What can I say, Ernie?—
Younger than my son, you are
nevertheless my old friend

whom I trust.

## vi Judy

You have the light step
of Ariel, the smile of Puck,
something of Rosalind's
courage, I think, though you are small
as I imagine Perdita to have been

(and why Shakespeare gets into all this at all
I don't know—but he does, insistently)

but when you set off alone, winter nights,
coat collar up, and in your pocket
that invisible flute,

it's myself I think of, 12 years old,
trudging home from the library lugging
too many books, and seeing

visions in Ilford High Road,

the passing faces oblivious
to all their own strange beauty under the street-lamps,

and I drunk on it.

## vii Lucy

Lucy taking
the family cat
along on her pilgrimage.

Lucy's nineteenth-century face
gazing steadfastly into the twenty first century.

Jewish Lucy
rooted in Emily's
New England fields.

Aquarian Lucy searching
for rhymes that dance,

for gestures that speak of
the rhyming seasons,

for the community
of poems and people.

**viii Margo**

The one who can't say it
says it.

The one who can't figure how
pictures what.

The song no one can sing
sounds, quiet
air in air.

**ix Mark**

Ripple of clear water
in the sun—inscape of moving, curling wavelets,
and the murmuring of them: an ideogram
for 'happiness'—

a buddha spring upwelling
in deep woods
where light must climb
down ladders of somber
needled branches.

## x Richard

i

The old poet, white-bearded
showing an antique motorcycle
to the children of the revolution.

The old poet overhearing
lovers telling one another poems,
and the poems are his.
His laugh rings out in sudden joy
as it did when he was twenty-one.
I hunger for a world
you can
live in forever.

ii

*'The very essence*
*of destiny hung over this house'*
(this time) *'and how was he,*
*a membrane stretched between the*
*light and darkness of the world,*
*not to become conscious of it?'*

I want
a world you can live in.

*'The blood ran to his head*
*and his heart beat like a trip-hammer*
*when he thought of*
*encountering the man,*
*of finding himself in his presence.*

*It was not cowardice; it was only that he had become*
*shudderingly aware of the tremendous task he*
*had undertaken*
*and when he had realized it completely,*
*to the very tips of his fingers and the depths of*
*his soul,*

*he smiled,*
*feeling rather like a man standing on the roof of*
*a burning house,*
*and marking*
*the spot on which he must without fail alight. . .*
*He must indeed be*
*a good jumper,*
*and something of a magician besides.'*

I want
a world.

**xi Roger**

'Mad prince'—OK—that's it—
a madness
of such simplicity
under the crown of
too much knowledge
(heavy on your head its
velvet and stupidly
glaring stones, as
on all our heads
that burden, all of us
weighed down with its despair)
that it lifts
out and through it

like your Jewish natural would escape
a rabbi's hat, and send it sailing
crazy into the sky
of pale funny blue like your eyes.

**xii Ted**

The people in you:
some are silent.

Two I see clear:

a girl at the edge of the sea
who dances in solitude
for joy at the sea's dance;
and she is one who speaks.

And an old man nearby
in a dark hut, who sits looking
into a pit of terror: hears
horror creeping upon the sea.
And he is silent.

Her voice lifts, silvery,
a flying shower in the sunlight

but the sky darkens, sea-music
twists into hideous tumult.
Other shadowy figures

move on the shore of my dream of you:
their lips form words but no sound
comes forth. None can speak

until the old man raises
his grim head and shouts
his curse or warning.

**xiii Vic**

The dog, Stalin, is free and foolish
as a holy hasid.
Wonder, arf, wonder wags his tail,
in him your soul
takes its rest and,
        twitching, sighing,
        lifting sensitive ears at odd noises,
grows.

## To Kevin O'Leary, Wherever He Is

Dear elusive Prince of Ireland,
I have received
from Arizona
your letter, with no return address
                                        but telling me
my name in Hebrew, and its meaning:
      entrance, exit,
      way through of
      giving and receiving,
      which are one.
Hallelujah! It's as if you'd sent me
in the U.S. mails
a well of water,
      a frog at its brim, and mosses;
sent me a cold and sweet freshness
dark to taste.
                              Love from the door,
                                        Daleth.

## The Day the Audience Walked Out on Me, and Why

*(May 8th, 1970, Goucher College, Maryland)*

Like this it happened:
after the antiphonal reading from the psalms
and the dance of lamentation before the altar,
and the two poems, 'Life at War' and
                                                            'What Were They Like?'
I began my rap,
and said:

Yes, it is well that we have gathered
in this chapel to remember
the students shot at Kent State,

but let us be sure we know
our gathering is a mockery unless
we remember also
the black students shot at Orangeburg two years ago,
and Fred Hampton murdered in his bed
by the police only months ago.

And while I spoke the people
—girls, older women, a few men—
began to rise and turn
their backs to the altar and leave.

And I went on and said,
Yes, it is well that we remember
all of these, but let us be sure
we know it is hypocrisy
to think of them unless
we make our actions their memorial,
actions of militant resistance.

By then the pews were almost empty
and I returned to my seat and a man stood up
in the back of the quiet chapel
(near the wide-open doors through which
the green of May showed, and the long shadows
of late afternoon)
and said my words
desecrated a holy place.

And a few days later
when some more students (black) were shot
at Jackson, Mississippi,
no one desecrated the white folks' chapel,
because no memorial service was held.

## Animal Rights

Pig and wasp are robbed of their names.
OK! Let brutal
Amerikan polizei
and tightassed DAR's be known forever
as pigs and wasps, but let's think up
new names for those we ripped off:

the roguish Black Berkshires, the intelligent
rangy ginger roamers of Mexican beaches,
Iowan acorn-eaters, fast on their small feet,
even the oppressed pink fatbacks in smelly
concentration-pens,
deserve a good name.

And the bees' ornery cousins—
oh, in the time of ripened pears,
of plum and fig burst open for very languor
of sweetness and juicy weight—
then you shall see the spiteful, buzzing, honeyless ones
graceful with ecstasy, clumsy with passion,
humble in pleasure no pale wasp
knows. What
shall their new name be?

## Leather Jacket

She turns, eager—
hand going out to touch
his arm. But touches
a cold thick sleeve.

*1970*

## The Needles

He told me about
a poem he was writing.
For me.

He told me it asked,
'When I mean only to brush her gently
with soft feathers,

do the feathers
turn into needles?'
His telling me

was a cloud of
soft feathers, I closed
my eyes and sank in it.

Many weeks
I waited. At last,
'Did you, were you able

to finish that poem
you told me about,
once?'

'No,' he said,
looking away.
Needles paused

for an instant on my skin
before they drew blood.

*1970*

## The Poem Unwritten

For weeks the poem of your body,
of my hands upon your body
    stroking, sweeping, in the rite of
    worship, going
    their way of wonder down
    from neck-pulse to breast-hair to level
    belly to cock–
for weeks that poem, that prayer,
unwritten.
        The poem unwritten, the act
left in the mind, undone. The years
a forest of giant stones, of fossil stumps,
blocking the altar.

*1970*

## The Good Dream

Rejoicing
because we had met again
we rolled laughing
over and over upon the big bed.

The joy was
not in a narrow sense
erotic—not
narrow in any sense.
It was

that all impediments,
every barrier, of history,
of learn'd anxiety,
wrong place and wrong time,

had gone down,
vanished.
It was the joy

of two rivers
meeting in depths of the sea.

*1970*

## Goethe's Blues

*(Fantasia on the*
Trilogie der Leidenschaft)

i

The hills stirring under their woven
leaf-nets, sighing, shimmering. . .
High summer.
                    And he with
April anguish tearing him,
heart a young animal, its fur
curly and legs too long.

But he is old. Sere.

'O love, O love,
not unkind,
kind,

my life goes out of me
breath by breath

thinking of your austere
compassion.'

ii

Fame tastes 'sweet' to him,
too sweet, and then sour,
and then not at all.

It is not a substance
to taste, it is a box
in which he is kept.

He is a silver
dandelion seed entrapped
in a cube of plexiglass.

**iii**

'Stop the coach! I want to get out
and die!'
            His friends
wonder what he's scribbling,
'furiously,' as it is said,
all the way back.
They're doing 80, the freeway's
all theirs.
            'Nature smiles,
and smiles, and
says nothing. And I'm
driving away from the gates of
Paradise.'

*1970*

## February Evening in Boston, 1971

The trees' black hair electric
brushed out,
            fierce haloes.

And westward
veils of geranium hold their own,
even yet. Transparent.

People are quickly, buoyantly
crossing the Common
into evening, into
a world of promises.

It was the custom of my tribe
to speak and sing;
not only to share the present, breath and sight,
but to the unborn.
Still, even now, we reach out
toward survivors. It is a covenant
of desire.

                    Shall there be, by long chance,
one to hear me after the great, the gross,
                                        the obscene silence,
to hear and wonder that in the last days
the seasons gave joy,
that dusk transmuted
                        brilliant pink to lilac, lilac
                        to smoke blue?

And lovers sat on a bench in the cold as night drew in,
laughing because the snow had melted.

## The Sun Going Down upon Our Wrath

You who are so beautiful–
your deep and childish faces,
your tall bodies–

Shall I warn you?

Do you know
what it was to have
a certitude of grasses waving
upon the earth though all
humankind were dust?
Of dust returning
to fruitful dust?

Do you already know
what hope is fading from us
and pay no heed,
see the detested grave-worm shrivel,
the once-despised,
and not need it?

Is there an odyssey
your feet pull you towards
away from now to walk
the waters, the fallen
orchard stars?
It seems
your fears are only the old fears, antique
anxieties, how graceful;
they lay as cloaks on shoulders
of men long dead,
skirts of sorrow wrapped
over the thighs of legendary women.

Can you be warned?

If you are warned will your beauty
scale off, to leave
gaping meat livid with revulsion?

No, who can believe it.
Even I in whose heart
stones rattle, rise each day
to work and imagine.

Get wisdom, get understanding, saith
the ancient. But he believed
there is nothing new under the sun,
his future
rolled away in great coils forever
into the generations.
Among conies the grass
grew again
and among bones.
And the bones would rise.

If there is time to warn you,
if you believed there shall be
never again a green blade in the crevice,
luminous eyes in rockshadow:
if you were warned and believed
the warning,

would your beauty
break into spears of fire,

fire to turn fire, a wall
of refusal, could there be
a reversal I cannot

hoist myself high enough
to see,
plunge myself deep enough
to know?

The gleam of thy drenched
floors of leaf-layers! Fragrance
of death and change!
                    If there is only
now to live, I'll live
the hour till doomstroke
crouched with the russet toad,
my huge human size
no more account than a bough fallen:

not upward,
searching for branch-hidden sky:
I'll look
down into paradise.

Thy moss gardens, the deep
constellations of green, the striate
rock furred with emerald,
inscribed with gold lichen,
with scarlet!
             Thy smooth
acorns in roughsurfaced
precise cups!
             Thy black
horns of plenty!

## Joie de Vivre

All that once hurt
(healed) goes on hurting
in new ways. One same heart
–not a transplant–
cut down to the stump
throbs, new, old.
Bring paper and pencil
out of the dimlit into
the brightlit room, make sure
all you say is true.
'Antonio, Antonio,
the old wound's
bleeding.' 'Let it bleed.'
The pulse of life-pain
strong again, count it,
fast but
not fluttering.

## The Wanderer

The chameleon who wistfully
thought it could not suffer
nostalgia

now on a vast sheet of clear glass
cowers, and prays for vision
of russet bark and trembling foliage.

## Brass Tacks

### i

The old wooden house a soft
almost-blue faded green
embowered in southern autumn's
nearly-yellow green leaves,
the air damp after a night of rain.

### ii

The black girl sitting alone in the back row
smiled at me.

### iii

Yes, in strange kitchens
I know where to find the forks,

and among another woman's perfume bottles
I can find the one that suits me,

and in the bedrooms
of children I have not met
I have galloped the island
of Chincoteague at 3 a.m., too tired to sleep–

but beyond that

at how many windows I have listened
to the cricket-quivering of borrowed moonlight.

iv

Brass tacks that glint
illumination of dailiness
and hold down feet to earth
ears to the rush and whisper of
the ring and rattle of
the Great Chain—

brass tacks that rivet
the eyes to Consolation,
that *are* Consolation.

v

Weighed down by two shopping bags she trudges
uphill diagonally across the nameless (but grassy)
East Boston square—Fort Something,
it was once. Her arms ache, she wonders
if some items she is carrying deserve to be classed
as conspicuous consumption. It would be nice
if a gray pet donkey came by magic
to meet her now, panniers ready
for her burdens. . . She looks up,
and the weight
lifts: behind the outstretched eager
bare limbs and swaying twigs of two
still-living elms

in moonstone blue of dusk
the new moon itself is swinging
back and forth on a cloud-trapeze!

vi

The spring snow
is flying
aslant
over the crocus gold
and into evening.

vii

Returning tired towards his temporary
lodging, wondering again
if his workday was useful at all

the human being saw the rose-colored leaves
of a small plant growing among
the stones of a low wall

unobtrusively, and found himself
standing quite still, gazing,
and found himself
smiling.

## The Old King

*for Jim Forest*

*The Soul's dark Cottage, batter'd and decay'd,*
*Lets in new Light through chinks that Time hath made.*

And at night—
the whole night a cavern, the world
an abyss—

lit from within:

a red glow
throbbing at the chinks.

Far-off a wanderer
unhoused, unhouseled,
wonders to see
hearthblaze:
fears, and takes heart.

## The Roamer

The world comes back to me
eager and hungry, and often
too tired to wag its tail,

a dog with wanderlust
back from South Boston or the Reservoir.

Keeps coming back,
brought by triumphant strangers
who don't understand he knows the way well.
Faint jingle of collartag breaking
my sleep, he arrives
and patiently scratches himself on the front steps.
I let in blue
daybreak,
in rushes the world,

visible dog concocted
of phantasmagoric atoms.
Nudges my hand with wet nose,
flumps down, deeply sighing,

smelling of muddy streams, of thrown-away treasures,
of some exotic news, not blood, not flowers,
and not his own fur—
unable
except by olifact
to tell me anything.
Where have I been
without the world? Why am I glad
he wolfs his food and gathers
strength for the next journey?

crossing furrows from green hedge to hedge,
rather a crawling out of one's deep hole

in midfield, in the moist
gray that is dawn, and begins

to hurt the eyes;
                    to sit on one's haunches
gazing, listening, picking up
the voices of wheat, trail of other
animals telling the nose the night's news.

To be at the hollow center of a field
at dawn; the radius
radiant. Silver
to gold, shadows
violet dancers.

                         By noon the builders
scream in, the horizon
blocks afternoon, a jagged
restlessness. To be
an animal dodging
pursuers it smells but can't
see clear, through labyrinths

of new walls. To be mangled or
grow wise in escape.
To bite, and destroy the net.

                    To make it maybe
into the last of day, and witness
crimson wings
                cutting down after
the sun gone down in wrath.

To stay perhaps,

one throat far-off
pulsing to venture
one note from its feathers,
one bell,

on into dewfall, into
peculiar silence.

The multitude gone, labyrinths
crumbling.
To go down
back into the known hole.

### Alice Transfixed

When your huge face
whipped by the highest branches
finds itself peering into a nest,
pathos of scraggly twigs and tiny eggs:

and the appalled mother-bird is shrieking
'Serpent! Serpent!' at you,
her beak grazing your ear–

that's when you wonder
if the first wish, the first question,
were worth it.
Mournfully
the feet you have bade-farewell-to
trample in cloudhidden thickets,
crushing the slow beasts.

## Memories of John Keats

*for Mitch*

*Watchfulness and sensation* as John Keats
said to me
for it was to me
he said it
          (and to you)

Side by side we lay full-length
upon a spumy rock, envisioning
Ailsa Craig

                    The sea tumult
bore away
          a word
     and a word

And again *that which is creative*
*must create itself* he said
We skirted
the murmurous green hollow
Vale of Health

strolling the spiral road, the
Vale of Soulmaking

He would stop to pluck
a leaf, finger
a stone

*watchfulness* was his word
*sensation*
          *and watchfulness in itself*
*the Genius*
*of Poetry must work out*
*its own salvation in a man*

*I leapt* he said
*headlong into the sea. . .*

Blue of Ireland quickens in the sea,
green fish
                    deep below the fathoms
of glass air.

My shadow
if I were floating free

would stroke the mountains' bristles
pensively, a finger of dark

smaller even than the plane's
tiny shadow, unnoticed,

nearing the edge of
                              the old world.

**By Rail through the Earthly Paradise, Perhaps Bedfordshire**

The fishermen among the fireweed.

Towpath and humpbacked bridge. Cows
in one field, slabs of hay
ranged in another.

Common day
precious to me.
There's nothing else
to grasp.

The train
moves me past it too fast, not much,
just a little, I don't want
to stay for ever.
                                        Horses,
three of them, flowing across a paddock
as wind flows over barley.

Oaks in parkland, distinct,
growing their shadows.
A man from Cairo across from me
reading *A Synopsis of Eye Physiology.*
The brickworks,
fantastical slender chimneys.

I'm not hungry,
not lonely. It seems
at times I want nothing,
no human giving and taking.
Nothing I see
fails to give pleasure,

no thirst for righteousness
dries my throat, I am silent
and happy, and troubled only
by my own happiness. Looking,

looking and naming. I wish the train now
would halt for me at a station in the fields,
(the name goes by
unread).
                    In the deep aftermath
of its faded rhythm, I could become

a carved stone
set in the gates of the earthly paradise,

an angler's fly
lost in the sedge to watch the centuries.

## The Cabbage Field

Both Taine and the inland English child
were mocked for their independent
comparison of the sea to a field of cabbages:

but does this field
of blue and green and purple curling
turmoil of ordered curves, reaching

out to the smoky twilight's immense
ambiguousness we call
*horizon,* resemble

anything but the sea?

## In Silence

Clear from the terraced mountainside
through fretwork of laden vines, red apples, brown
heavy pears poised to fall, and not falling,
I saw a woman deep in the valley
wrapped in a blue cloak as if autumn
veiled in the ripe sun
were running its cutting-edge over her skin,
hurry from her house out to the garden swimming pool
and bend to greet a child there, and again hurry
round the pool to the far side,
and drop the cloak from her shoulders,
kick off her shoes in haste
and at last slowly, smoothly,
flowingly as if all her being
were blue water,
enter the blue water.

*Brunnenburg, 1971*

## To Antonio Machado

Here in the mountain woods
a furious small fountain
is channelled through pipes of hollow sapling
into a great wooden vat bevelled with moss,
and thence brims over into a concrete cistern
and from the cistern quietly
in modest rills
into the meadow where cows graze
and fringed wild carnations, white and sweet,
grow by the path.
Machado,
old man,
dead man,
I wish you were here alive
to drink of the cold, earthtasting, faithful spring,
to receive the many voices
of this one brook,
to see its dances
of fury and gentleness,
to write the austere poem
you would have known in it.

*Brunnenburg, 1971*

## Sun, Moon, and Stones

'I longed to go away, to take to the desolate, denuded mountains opposite me and walk and walk, without seeing anything but sun, moon, and stones.'

—*Nikos Kazantzakis*

Sun
moon
stones
        but where shall we find
        water?

Sun
    hoists all things upward and outward
    thrusts
    a sword of thirst into the mouth.

Moon
    fills the womb with ice.

Stones: weapons that carry
        warmth into night
        dew into day, and break
        the flesh of stumbling feet.

And we were born to that sole end:
    to thirst and grow
    to shudder
    to dream in lingering dew, lingering warmth
    to stumble searching.

But O the fountains,
    where shall we find them.

## Man Alone

When the sun goes down, it writes
a secret name in its own blood for remembrance,
the excess of light
an ardor slow to cool:
and man has time to seek shelter.

But when the moon
gains the horizon, though it tarries
a moment, it vanishes
without trace of silver

and he is left with the stars only,
fierce and remote, and not revealing
the stones of the dark roads.

So it is with the gods,
and with the halfgods,
and with the heroes.

## Road

The wayside bushes waiting, waiting.
There's no one,
no one to meet them.
Golden in my sunset dustcloud
I too pass by.

A glimpsed world, halfway through the film,
one slow shot of a ward at night

holds me when the rest is quickly
losing illusion. Strange hold,

as of romance, of glamor: not because
even when I lived in it I had

illusions about that world: simply because
I did live there and it was

a world. Greenshaded lamp glowing
on the charge desk, clipboards
stacked on the desk for the night,

sighs and waiting, waiting-for-morning stirrings
in the dim long room, warm, orderly,
and full of breathings as a cowbarn.

Death and pain dominate this world, for though
many are cured, they leave still weak,

still tremulous, still knowing mortality
has whispered to them; have seen in the folding
of white bedspreads according to rule

the starched pleats of a shroud.
It's against that frozen
counterpane, and the knowledge too
how black an old mouth gaping at death can look

that the night routine has in itself—
without illusions—glamor, perhaps. It had

a rhythm, a choreographic decorum:
when all the evening chores had been done

and a multiple restless quiet listened
to the wall-clock's pulse, and turn by turn

the two of us made our rounds
on tiptoe, bed to bed,

counting by flashlight how many pairs
of open eyes were turned to us,

noting all we were trained to note,
we were gravely dancing—starched

in our caps, our trained replies,
our whispering aprons—the well-rehearsed

pavanne of power. Yes, wasn't it power,
and not compassion,
                                        gave our young hearts
their hard fervor? I hated

to scrub out lockers, to hand out trays of
unappetizing food, and by day, or the tail-end of night

(daybreak dull on gray faces—ours and theirs)
the anxious hurry, the scolding old-maid bosses.
But I loved the power
of our ordered nights,

gleaming surfaces I'd helped to polish
making patterns in the shipshape
halfdark–
loved
the knowing what to do, and doing it,
list of tasks getting shorter

hour by hour. And knowing
all the while that Emergency
might ring with a case to admit, anytime,

if a bed were empty. Poised,
ready for that.
The camera
never returned to the hospital ward,

the story moved on into the streets,
into the rooms where people lived.

But I got lost in the death rooms a while,
remembering being (crudely, cruelly,

just as a soldier or one of the guards
from Dachau might be) in love with order,

an angel like the *chercheuses de poux,* floating
noiseless from bed to bed,

smoothing pillows, tipping
water to parched lips, writing

details of agony carefully into the Night Report.

## At the 'Mass Ave Poetry Hawkers' Reading in the Red Book Cellar

When even craning my neck
I couldn't see over and round
to where poems were sounding from

I found eyesight wasn't so utterly
my way of being
as I'd supposed: each voice

was known to me, I could name
each, and conjure seven
faces, seven heads of

mysteriously intense and living
hair, curly, wavy, straight, dark, light,
or going further, *not* conjure

any picture: solely hear
person in voice: further:
to listen deeper:

deep listening: into the earth
burrowing, into the water courses
hidden in rockbed.

And songs from these
beloved strangers, these close friends,
moved in my blind illumined head,
songs of terror, of hopes unknown to me,
terror, dread: songs of knowledge, songs
of their lives wandering

out into oceans.

*1972*

## Small Satori

Richard's lover has the look,
robust and pure, of a nineteenth-century
Russian heroine. Surely her brows and chin,
smooth hair, free walk,
                                        and the way she can sit poised and quiet,
speak of depth.

                                    Across the room
his profile—all I can see
beyond the range of heads and shoulders,
in smoke, in candlelight—
looks off into inner distance,
poignant, a little
                                    older than last year,
still very young though.

I think she is watching him too.

Calmly, calmly, I am seeing them both.
Reassured.

*1972*

## The Life around Us

*for David Mitchell and David Hass*

Poplar and oak awake
all night. And through
all weathers of the days of the year.
There is a consciousness
undefined.
Yesterday's twilight, August
almost over, lasted, slowly changing,
until daybreak. Human sounds
were shut behind curtains.
No human saw the night in this garden,
sliding blue into morning.
Only the sightless trees,
without braincells, lived it
and wholly knew it.

## Knowing the Way

The wood-dove utters
slowly
        those words he has
to utter,
and softly.
            But takes flight
boldly,
and flies fast.

## Notes

About two thirds of the poems in this volume were written concurrently with the 'notebook' poem that gave its name to my last book, *To Stay Alive.* The rest were written—some in England during the summer of 1971—since then, except for a few which got 'lost' during the compilation of earlier volumes.

PAGE

1 'Hut'—This poem is a pendant to the poem 'Relearning the Alphabet.'

7 '*L'homme est . . ./en lui-même*'—'Humans are strange creatures, whose center of gravity lies outside their own body.' These words are by the French poet Francis Ponge (1899–).

10 'Time to Breath'—adapted from an untitled prose poem in *Ombres,* by Jean-Pierre Burgart (Mercure de France, Paris, 1965).

11 'Hunza'—residents of a small mountain kingdom in northwest Kashmir, noted for their health and longevity.

12 'M. C. 5'—the rock group associated with the White Panthers in Motor City. John Sinclair: poet, revolutionary, sometime political prisoner. The poem was written while listening to the record album *Kick Out the Jams* during the moon-landings.

23 '*Richard* (ii)'—the quoted lines are adapted from *The Maurizius Case,* by Jakob Wasserman (1928).

38 'Antonio, Antonio,/the old wound's/bleeding.'—a quote from 'Cranach,' in Sir Herbert Read's *Collected Poems* (Faber and Faber, London, 1946; New Directions, New York, 1951).

41 The italicized lines are from Edmund Waller (1606–87).

43 'Life Is Not a Walk across a Field'—Boris Pasternak, from a Russian proverb.

44 'Alice Transfixed'—see Chapter V of Lewis Carroll's *Alice in Wonderland.*

45 The italicized words are all quotes from John Keats's letters, as in the phrase 'the Vale of Soulmaking.' The 'Vale of Health' is a part of Hampstead Heath, London, near which the poet lived.

48 'Both Taine and the inland English child'—H. A. Taine was the French literary historian (1828–93), while the 'English child' is mentioned in an essay by G. K. Chesterton.

49 Antonio Machado—Spanish poet (1875–1939).

54 '*chercheuses de poux*'—a reference to the poem 'The Women Hunting Lice' by Arthur Rimbaud (1854–91). The prose translation by Anthony Hartley in *The Penguin Book of French Verse,* Volume III, begins: 'When the child's brow full of red torments begs for the white swarm of lazy dreams, tall charming sisters with delicate fingers and silvery nails come near his bed."